Journeys in Verse: A Poetic Expedition

Isha Liaqat

BookLeaf Publishing

India | USA | UK

Presentation by *BookLeaf Publishing*

Web: www.bookleafpub.com

E-mail: info@bookleafpub.com

ISBN: 9789360949990

First edition 2024

To those who wander the corridors of emotion,

to the dreamers, the seekers, and the lovers of words,

this collection is dedicated to you.

For my family,

whose love is the heartbeat that resonates through these verses.

You are the anchors that ground me in the storms of creativity.

To my friends,

the fellow travellers on this poetic expedition.

Your laughter, tears, and shared moments are the ink that colours these pages.

In memory of Nani,

whose spirit lingers in the spaces between the lines.

Your presence, though missed, is felt in the cadence of every word.

To the unsung heroes,

whose stories are woven into the fabric of these poems.

May your journeys find echoes in the hearts of those who read.

This collection is a tapestry of shared experiences,

a celebration of the human spirit,

and a tribute to the beauty found in the journey of life.

ACKNOWLEDGEMENT

In the tapestry of creating "Journeys in Verse: A Poetic Expedition," I find myself indebted to the warmth and support of those who have been integral to this literary journey.

To my family, the steadfast pillars of my life, your unwavering encouragement and understanding have been the bedrock of my creative endeavours. Your love is the muse that breathes life into these verses for you are the ones that have taught me to seek out these experiences. Your support is etched into the very fabric of this collection.

A heartfelt thank you to my friends, whose camaraderie and shared experiences have shaped the narratives within these poems. Your laughter, tears, and shared moments have been the ink that colours the pages of this collection.

To the readers, who embark on this journey with open hearts, your presence gives purpose to these verses. May these poems find resonance in your own experiences and kindle the flames of reflection.

Finally, to the voice within, who whispers inspiration in the quiet moments and paints vivid scenes in the canvas of my mind, thank you for the endless gifts of creativity.

This collection is a shared endeavour, and each of you has played an integral part in its creation. "Journeys in Verse" is as much yours as it is mine.

With heartfelt gratitude,

Isha Liaqat

PREFACE

Welcome, dear reader, to "Journeys in Verse: A Poetic Expedition." As you embark on this literary voyage, you are not merely turning pages; you are stepping into a world where words become vessels, carrying you across the diverse landscapes of the human experience.

In these verses, penned by the soulful hand of Isha, every word is a footfall on the path of emotion, every line a contour of the heart's terrain. The title, "Journeys in Verse," is more than a collection of words—it is an invitation to explore, to wander through the echoes of shared moments, and to connect with the timeless narratives that bind us all.

Within these pages, you will encounter tributes to the pillars of life in "For Mom" and "For Dad," feel the weight of wars waged and the yearning for tranquility, and witness the dance of betrayal and the solace of faith. Themes unfold like petals, revealing the ethereal landscapes of dreams, the pursuit of happiness, the cyclical nature of life, and the enduring tapestry of memories.

As we traverse this poetic expedition, remember that each poem is a vessel—a vessel crafted to carry you beyond the confines of the ordinary. These verses are bridges between worlds, illuminating the shadows, and celebrating the luminous threads that connect us in our shared humanity.

May this collection be more than a mere reading experience; may it be a reflection, an introspection, and a celebration of the profound beauty found within the human spirit. Join the expedition, navigate the heart's compass, and let these verses guide you through the timeless landscapes of emotion.

Your journey begins now.

For Mom

Blessed to have you.
Grateful to have you.
Words aren't enough to describe you.

Through the highs and the lows,
The laughs and the tears,
Your unwavering presence has been my anchor.

Unshakeable, Strong and Loving.

From cradle through youth, you've taught me.
Through my teenage years, you disciplined me.
But, through it all you've never forgotten to love
me.

Supportive, Patient and Whole-hearted.

The sacrifices, the long hours, the lectures.
All of them sincere.
All of them for us.

Selfless, Inspiring and Truly Extraordinary.

The effort, the love, the support.
The nurture, the warmth, the protection.

Bountiful and endless.

Beautiful, Elegant and Caring.

The hugs and the kisses.
The good times.
The simplicity of the sunlit coffee chats.

Invaluable, Moving and Forever Treasured.

The driving force behind my motivation.
The silent architect of my success.
The reason behind my happiness.

For Dad

Your teachings and your words of wisdom,
Have allowed us to flourish.

Your time and your caring nature,
Have allowed us to grow and prosper.

The dedication and the commitment,
For our growth and future.

The early mornings and the long nights,
The movies and the dinners,
The time in your company provides comfort like
no other.

Through our hardships and successes you've
been there,
A standing pillar of protection.
Your composure stronger than ever.

The silent prayers,
The safety under your shadow,
The sturdy hand when we fall,
You've been there through it all.

Your quiet strength, Heroic

Your caring nature, Sincere
Your guidance and your support, like no other.

The inspiration behind my motivation.
The guardian of my success.
The heartbeat of my happiness.

Echoes Of Eternity: Embracing the Seasons of Time

Winter arrives, snow cascading, a cup o' hot
choca in hand.
New year, new dreams, new goals unfold,
A fresh chapter in the story of life.

Spring emerges, a season of growth and new
beginnings,
Hope blooms in vibrant hues.

Summer welcomes the sun's warmth, smiles all
around,
Beach trips and flights across the skies,
Holidays painted with memories.

Autumn sets in, cosy with hot drinks and
warmth,
Long walks late after dusk.

Time filters by, each year a layer added to the
tapestry of age.
The present fading into the past, the future
drawing nearer.

Nostalgia whispers of the good old days,
Dreams of the past weaving through the lens of
memory.
Proud of the journey, for it shapes who we are.

Trapped in the allure of tomorrow, forgetting the
gift of today,
Days transforming into months, months melding
into years.

Time, a fickle yet driving force.
Pushing, steering, rewarding our journey.

Stars twinkle above, guiding in the darkness,
A celestial light through the ebb and flow of life.

A deep breath,a blissful sleep,
A cycle, a rhythm repeats…

Echoes Across Time: Yesterday's Footprints, Today's Endeavours, Tomorrow's Hopes

The trials of the past.
The successes of the present.
The hopes for the future.

The times that have gone, are now behind us,
Yet, the lessons we learn and messages they
leave are forever dear.

The times we live in today, are what prepare us
for tomorrow,
But, more importantly are the ones that allow us
to touch new horizons.

The times that are yet to come are only too near,
They allow us to pursue our dreams and learn to
never fear.

The past shapes us to be who we are,
Yet the present forces us to learn and evolve,
While the future reminds us to never neglect all
that we've sowed.

The moments in the past teach us to never falter,
While the present gives us abundant
opportunities to alter,
And the future is but a gift of the effort of our
endeavour.

The tales untold, part wisdom.
The stories of today, craft new starts.
A testament of resilience to those who dare.

Time is precious and life too short.

Live in the moment and treasure what is in our
grasp,
For tomorrow isn't promised and the past is
already clasped.

Echoes of Sorrow: War's Unending Tale

In the silence, cries echo.
Tears stream like rivers,
Souls wander in search.

Veiled in shadows, brutal truths lurk.

Harsh realities exhale.
Blood spilled immeasurably.
Truth silenced, carried with the passing wind.

Bombs dropped like rain.
Rubble and debris litter the street.
Tyranny reigns supreme.

Quaking and in fear, people are coerced to
accept evil.
Quaking and in fear, injustice is enforced.
Quaking and in fear, cruelty wins.

No refuge.
No safety.
No mercy.

Children in pain and fear.

Shattered and broken.
Strayed and orphaned.

Ambitions shredded.
Dreams torn asunder.
Happiness pierced by sorrow

Stripped of their peace.
Tranquillity a distant memory.

Families torn apart.
Unborns perish before birth.
All stripped of their inherent rights.

No refuge.
No safety.
No mercy.

Day in, Day out
With the wake of a new day,
Survival questioned,
Answers elusive.

As the dusk settles, dreams emerge
Of justice prevailing,
Of peace reclaiming its throne,
Of an end to this torture.

The hope persists today and forever.

Echoes of Distrust: Betrayal's Embrace

Intentions veiled, concealed behind counterfeit
smiles.
Truth eclipsed by a web of lies.
The jealousy justified.

More traps laid, more curve balls hurled.
The relentless game rages on.

Lies and deception intertwine,
Malice and hate, spreading faster than wildfire.

Incessant disapproval, eyes aflame with
contempt,
The cycle perpetuates, dissonance ever present.

Use and abuse, a daily recurrence,
Betrayal and falsehood eternally entwined.

Leeches suck harder, vying for the apex.
Yet, the game knows no end.

Glancing over my shoulder with each cautious
step,
Anger simmers through my veins.

Who needs enemies when 'family' bears the
knife?
Who needs enemies when 'friends' dance with
duplicity?

Echoes of The End: Lost in the Maze of Life

From birth to death,
From the cradle to the grave,
Life is but a mere second.

As days progress into years,
Childhood into adulthood,
Time begins to fade away.

Youth matures with the dreams of wealth and
success.
Adults live with the resonance of responsibilities
trying to progress.
Elders living with the ghosts of the past- the
memories in excess.

Lost in the pursuit of tomorrow,
We often forget to be grateful for today,
But, life goes on.

Its finite nature fools us.
Its hardships strengthen us.
The experience transforms us.

Life's melody composed in a cyclical trance.

Nurturing, Breaking, Healing.

Our quest to survive the story before the end.

An hourglass that is ever nearing its finale,
Yet, the anticipation of a new chapter remains.

Echoes of Sound : Rising Beyond the Shadows

Through hardships and strife,
We stand unwavering, refusing to yield.

Through silent battles,
Defying defeat, we won't let them triumph.

Through the veil of sadness and trials,
Persist, keep moving forward.

Step by determined step,
Day by relentless day,
We forge strength from within.

Conquer the grief.
Defy the string of betrayal.
Break the silence that shackles.

Declare your worth,
Refuse to be walked upon.

Work diligently, let achievements speak,
Don't let them quell your shine.

Make yourself proud,

Ignore the noise around.

Your worth it,
Don't let doubt dictate otherwise.

Radiance in Shadows: A tribute to the 'Real' Ones

In the vast darkness, beacons of light emerge,
Guiding hands that lift you when you stumble
and fall.

The ones that accept you as you are,
And push you to reach for the stars.

The ones that bring out the best in you,
Always present, a reassuring presence near.

Thoughtful souls, precious and rare,
Their faces, radiant with the glow of care.

Their company, a haven full of warmth,
The time with them short, yet special.

In the tapestry of shared love and joy,
Conversations that delve into the depths of the
soul.

Words of motivation, a sturdy support,
Laughter and smiles, games and fun.

Secrets shared and hugs exchanged.

Silent admiration- a language spoken beyond
words.

Moments dripping with love, pure and genuine.
Understanding, an unspoken bond that
transcends.

Each second with them is a treasure,
Everyday more bearable, thanks to their
presence.

Let us hold them close, for they are rare gems,
One in a million, these lights in the darkness.

The Haunting Shadows: Unveiling Evil's Veil

Around us, malevolence coils like a serpent,
A whisper, a trickster, a malevolent ploy.

Illusions, potent and beguiling,
Threats looming, casting a daunting shadow.
Danger, a sinister spectre lurking.

Mayhem and madness, an engulfing tempest,
Residing in every nook and cranny, high and
low.

Within and without, deception wears a cunning
mask,
Betraying trust time and again, a cycle of bitter
surprise.

An invitation, appealing,
Yet, consequences, dire and unforgiving.

Crime is rife.
These times are anything but nice.

Danger lurking ever nearer.
The risk, far greater.

Darkness cloaks, concealing sinister intent,
While light bears witness to the encroaching
abyss.

Evil expands, an ominous force,
Seeking. Feasting. Manifesting.

Tainted Integrity: The Stench of Corruption

Corruption infiltrates n' spreads
Over and over, manipulations occur,
Right under our unsuspecting noses,
Right within the walls of our homes.
Uses you and leaves you stranded,
Power and money, the sinister origin,
Trust shattered one too many times.
Intents of harm fueled by greed.
On it goes,
Never to cease…

Emancipation: From Suffering to Freedom

The scars burn bright- a reminder or a trophy?

Shackles tighten their grip, a suffocating
embrace.

Torment grinds on, wilder, fiercer.

Truth unveiled, a canvas painted in fifty shades
of red.

A picture-perfect world, shrouded in dishonesty
and corruption.

Trust in only yourself- everyone else would love
to see you drown.

It's time to shatter the chains of pain, escape the
torment.

Soar beyond reality and inhale a fresh breath.

Break free of the shackles that try to ground you.

Let your passion ignite your way.

Freedom awaits.

Grateful for Blessings: A Journey of Thankfulness

Blessings abundant,
Both small and grand.

In the delicacies we savour,
The liquids we sip.
The fabrics we wear.

Above our head, sheltering dreams
In a place we call home, where safety gleams.

The beauty of nature,
Like an artwork, that never ceases to please.

Within ourselves, a radiant glow,
The light that persists, an inner rainbow.

The ones we love, always kept near.
The ones we've met and those to come.
They give us a clear message to learn from.

Rewards for efforts, treasures we hold.
In the stories written, and tales untold.

The rise after a fall, endurance we find.

Through every challenge, strength defined.

Our wealth and health, our dignity and sanity.
Our peace and comfort, the tapestry of humanity.

One for all, and all for one,
In the symphony of life, where blessings are
spun.

Grateful Glimmers: Nature's Art

The colours we see,
The scents we smell,
The sounds we hear.

The nature of beauty encompasses us all around.
It soothes. It heals. It astounds.
Perfection in every hue and sound.

The tweets and chirps, music to our ears.
Full of songs, that eliminate fears.

The fragrance of the flowers, pleasant to the
nose.
Like perfumes of honey and rose.

The myriad of colours, beautiful beyond sight.
A canvas of wonders, day and night.

Raindrops dance, a tranquill theme.
The sun's warmth, a gentle gleam.

In the embrace of fresh, cool air,
Nature's beauty beyond compare.

Dawn births life, amidst the colours bright.
Dusk unfurls dreams in soft twilight.

Nature's poetry, a timeless rhyme.
A masterpiece echoing through time.

Guiding Light: Finding Faith and Purpose

A compass to life.

Your faith, a soothing balm for worries,
A beacon of hope on the darkest days,
A sacred space to release your thoughts.

It lifts you up when no-one else can,
A safe space to cry your eyes out.

A path paved with peace and internal
tranquillity.

Truth, a compass leading to meaning,
The destination preordained.

Morals and teachings for every step of the way,
If only we make the effort to integrate.

A message resonates- Unity and Peace.

Sunnah teachings of the beloved,
His life- a lesson to glean from.

The beautiful words that have guided many,

A manual for navigating life.

The essence lies in Peace with God, oneself, and
with His creation.
Through good intention and accepting His
guidance.

Begin the day with Bismillah.
End the day with Alhumdulilah.

His endless majesty and compassion
unparalleled.

The mercy of our Lord, His kindness and
forgiveness,
Prompt us to repent and seek His favour.

A life in His obedience is one of eternal treasure.

Faith-
A protector, a guide,
Unfaltering, ever true.

Rising from the Ashes: Defying Defeat

Sadness, an unexpected guest in life's great
tapestry,
Envelops us momentarily, a fleeting shadow in
existence.

Failure, an uneasy companion in life's intricate
path.
Curveballs and obstacles, the trials urging us to
rise.

Only after conquering defeat, does victory
unveil its radiant face.
Only after embracing the sadness, can light
emerge from the shadows.

Life's unfortunate stages of life, a crucible
testing, strengthening, and imparting wisdom,
Transforming the fruits of our labour into a
nectar of profound sweetness.

Don't beat yourself down during the low times,
For they too shall pass with the coming of time.

Moving on and learning from the experience,

The most valuable souvenir of life.

Learning and growing is all part of the process.
Each challenge, a brushstroke contributing to the
masterpiece.

Yes, it is daunting. Yes, it challenges us.
Yes, yielding may seem easier, though the finish
line looms nearer.

How enchanting to witness the culmination of
effort just beyond our grasp.
We stand on the precipice, almost there. Keep
pressing on.

Better days will unfold. Resolutions will
manifest.
Things will work out.

Chasing the Stars: Achieving Heights

Dream expansively.
Reap the rewards.
Enjoy the journey, relish the process.
All day, everyday, today n' tomorrow, until
victory's in our hands.
Make it happen- don't wait to initiate.

Get up and prepare. Now's the time to
commence.
Open the door. Wander into the realm of
adventures you've envisioned.
Admire the possibilities, aim with precision,
achieve with determination.
Learn to live in the moment and love the journey
you're on.
Search far and wide, for the opportunities are
endless.

A little effort everyday speaks volume;
dedication is the key to inevitable success.
Cross those days out- we're on the path to
triumph.
Quit the bad habits early and start with the new.

Understand the impossible is possible and you're
already on the precipice.
It's time to shine brighter.
Reflect on your path. Respect the journey.
Repeat the process.
Earn it for you really do deserve it.
Dream it today, make it reality tomorrow.

Rise and Shine: The Path to Success

Habits and consistency, the key to unlock potential. Start today and let the momentum keep you going.
Aim high. Achieve. Accomplish. Life unfolds as an adventure; embrace risks, for there lies growth.
Prosper in silence, cultivating passion with patience for good things take time.
Pray for guidance, Seek inner peace and persist with unwavering determination. Let positivity light your path.
Inquire, Inspire Imagine- the trinity of creativity and progress.
Never surrender to self-doubt. You are your greatest asset.
Enjoy every moment, love it, live with purpose. Study diligently, Rest well and let your brilliance shine.
Strive relentlessly to be a better version of yourself; success awaits at the next destination.

Memories' Chime: A Cheerful Nostalgia

Memories breathe nostalgia and grace,
Of times of greatness and craze.

Memories resurface time and again,
Of innocence riding in childhood's train.

Memories bittersweet,
In times of loss and grief.

Memories carefree and wild,
In adventures and of travels in style.

Memories gratifying and full of pride,
Of achievements and milestones side by side.

Memories captivated in past and present's
embrace,
Celebrating the beauty in ordinary grace.

Memories relived, in snapshots of time.
Memories relived, during life's climb.

Harmony Unveiled:
Shielding, Blooming, and
Finding Serenity

Craft a mental refuge, a haven secure,
A line of protection, a tranquil allure.

Invest in inner peace, let it bloom.
Growth and boundaries, your personal room.

Take time to yourself, in solace dwell ,
Reflect amid times of quiet, where your thoughts
swell.

Balance and blend, life's intricate art,
Savour the mend, let healing impart.

Resilience, an ingredient in your brew.
A tool for triumph, adversity through.

Well-being, a fusion of body and mind
Transform choices, self-care designed.

Write your narrative, an adventure unfurled.
In the vast expanse, your story, your world.

Against All Tides: Surviving the Unknown

Shield and protect. Strive to achieve.
Unite in hardship if in need, together through
adversity.

Recall the trials, the lessons of each endeavour.
Vanquish today, so tomorrow doesn't fear.

Invest in your survival, navigate the rough.
Vacate the mind, let go of stress, be tough.

Alone in solitude, find the power to overcome
Learn to live or live to learn, choices become.